Inspirmaetions

INSPIRATIONAL POETRY

Dr. Mae Hicks Jones

Order this book online at www.trafford.com
or email orders@trafford.com

Most Trafford titles are also available at major online book retailers.

Printed in the United States of America.

ISBN: 978-1-4269-2720-1 (sc)

Trafford rev. 01/22/2011

 www.trafford.com

North America & international
toll-free: 1 888 232 4444 (USA & Canada)
phone: 250 383 6864 ♦ fax: 812 355 4082

Dedicated to my daughter, Brittney and my late mother, Rose.
Through you I found me, you make me better! I love You!

Contents

FOR THE DETERMINED   1

AMAEZING 1   3

ACHIEVE   5

LIFE   7

LOVE   9

PEACE   11

POISED   13

THE TEST OF TIME!   15

VOICE   17

IDENTITY   19

BLACK TIES   21

KNOW YOUR HISTORY   23

MISS AFRICAN-AMERICAN   26

LEGACY   28

FAMILY   31

CHILD'S PLAY   33

FAMILY   35

FAMILY REUNION   38

SHE IS   41

SPECIAL OCCASIONS   43

DAD   45

HAPPY FATHER'S DAY... TO MY MOTHER!   46

MOTHER   49

WORDS OF ENCOURAGEMENT   51

DECISIONS   53

I'VE BEEN IN THE STORM TOO LONG   55

WE ALL FALL DOWN   58

MUSIC SOOTHES THE SOUL!   60

SMELL THE FLOWERS   61

SPIRITUAL CORNER   63

IN MY FATHER'S HOUSE   65

REMEMBER ME   65

DIVERSITY   67

THE DIVERSITY CHALLENGE   69

TEACHING DIVERSE STUDENTS   72

DEARLY DEPARTED   75

STOP!   77

WHAT WILL IT TAKE?   79

WOMEN   81

WOMEN!   83

JUST BECAUSE YOU'RE YOU   85

IN APPRECIATION OF YOU!   87

FOR THE HOME   89

ON HER SIDE   91

ON HIS SIDE   92

THIS THRONE!   93

WELCOME!   94

NEW BEGINNING   95

THE END   97

FOR THE
DETERMINED

AMAEZING 1

How do you face the world after life has let you down,
Do you lift your head and laugh it off or continue to wear a frown?

You see life has thrown so many curve balls throughout the years,
You have to laugh to keep from crying and always face your fears.

Facing each day has been a challenge and as you all know,
Facing challenges head on makes a difference but move slow.

Slow enough so you understand what you have gone through,
But moving forward with your efforts and continue to be you.

Despite life's dilemmas keep your dreams alive,
For this won't last always and you will thrive.

Dream big and dream often and be a member of the few,
That is touched by divine order and you know this is true.

For he will never let you go and he gave his only son,
And based on popular demand he is the Amaezing 1.

ACHIEVE

Today is the day that you will achieve,
I know you can do it because you believe.
You know everything in life is what you make of it,
But it is difficult to achieve if you give up and quit.
You have to start and make a move,
To accomplish your goals you have to stay in the groove.
God gives you strength even when you're tired,
He uplifts the spirit and get you wired.
But the first move is yours and to get success,
You have to think wise and do your best.
For your best can take you anywhere,
So get up, push forward because I know you care.
In order to be in control of your destiny,
You must strive to be all that you can be.

LIFE

Life has its way of telling you a story,
Of your very own life's struggles and glory.
God knows your heart and how your life will be,
But you start your story that becomes your eulogy.
One day you could be happy and then the next day sad,
You could be laughing and then get mad.
Bad news happens one day and good news the next,
No matter what the situation keep it in context.
Look adversity in the eye and take life one day at a time,
For trials don't last forever and you'll know all the signs.
Signs provide insight of what is yet to come,
It takes your focus off one thing so you can focus on some.
So don't check out because one things for sure,
That you will be healed because there is a cure.
You may not take medicine for the situation you're in,
Because it's all how you manage and where you have been.
So take a walk in someone else's shoes before you judge them,
Then look at your life and think of a Hymn.
When you think back to all of the days gone by,
You can laugh, reflect and sometimes cry.
Because you've been thrown curve balls and lost some games,
For in the field of life the rules aren't the same.
So keep moving onward and whenever you're pushed,
Take heed and keep moving for this is no ambush.
For the force that is pushing you can only be defined,
As divine intervention that will strengthen your mind.

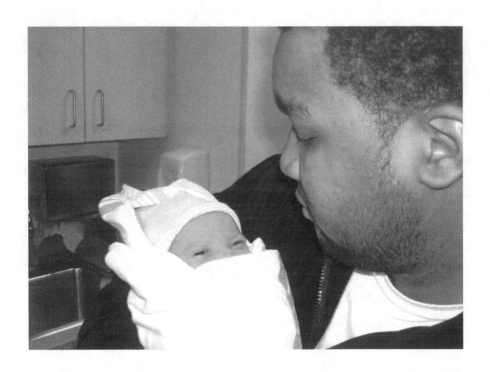

LOVE

Love has made us happy and it has made us sad,
It feels really good but it could make you mad.
You can love so hard that you could lose yourself,
It could overtake your life and your potential wealth.
But never give up your values and level of respect,
To be with someone who may put you in check.
For love isn't mean nor is it control,
It doesn't dictate your life or give you a role.
It doesn't hurt you nor does it desert you,
For love realizes you are a person too.
Love helps you when you're hurt and dries your eye,
Love is there for you when others make you cry.
Don't mistake love for infatuation, they are not the same,
Just like football and chess are two different games.
Love yourself first and then give love to someone,
It could be a treasured moment and so much fun.
For God so loved the world that he gave his only son,
He did this for you so that you are number one.
Love provides the passion and many other things,
Not like a one-night stand or a simple fling.
So recognize that love enriches your life,
Not add additional worry, struggles, stress and strife.
So if you find love hold on tight,
It'll be a great time and an excellent flight.

PEACE

I ran into an old friend that I had not seen for so long,
The closer I approached her I knew something was wrong.

For the first time in a long time we had time to talk,
So we hugged and smiled and started to walk.

I asked how she was doing and she began to cry,
She said there are times that it would be easier to just die.

She continued to say that she has so much anxiety,
Because problems are plentiful and they come in varieties.

As she continued her story there was one problem after another,
She said life was so overwhelming and she felt smothered.

I let her continue to speak and didn't find her life odd,
But when she finished her story I told her to seek God.

I told her that I didn't have all the answers but whenever I speak,
It is the Lord that gives me guidance and all the refuge I seek.

It is then that I manage problems better and some of my problems cease,
Because the Lord leads me to serenity and to all of my **PEACE**.

POISED

Stand up straight and look eye to eye,

To any person as you walk by.

Speak clearly to all and have confidence,

For you know you're strong and have good sense.

Be firm and diligent, it is not a chore,

As you reach your goals like an eagle you'll soar.

When you stand show the world who your are,

A gifted, bright and talented super star.

For you are making your mark on this earth,

You've took the challenge since your birth.

So stand up straight and make some noise,

But when you stand do it with poise.

THE TEST OF TIME!

I may not know rocket science,
Or be part of a major alliance.
I've never read hieroglyphics,
Or discussed mathematics and be specific.
I could not write a best-selling book,
Because I lacked the thought it took.
History was not a favorite subject,
And chemistry was like a foreign object.
I did not obtain the major degrees,
Or aspire to cross the seven seas.
What I learned I learned from living,
The art of being respectful and giving.
To see the world and the people in it,
And where I could have a place and benefit.
I respect everyone because I can go far,
For my love for people is as bright as a star,
The days that I've lived have taught me much,
About this world and not to be a crutch.
I've lived by the truth and that's all I need,
To establish myself and to take heed.
Yes, I'm living a life with zest,
I've paid my dues and passed each test.
I am a survivor and yes, I shine,
Because with this trait I pass the test of time!

VOICE

I've always been told that I had a place,
From the time I was a child that's been the case.
Adults would say, "Children should be seen and not heard,"
No matter what setting this was the final word.
Even as a silhouette it was the voice that I lacked,
Even as a shadow they knew I was black.
And so I kept quiet for days, years and yes even decades,
I never spoke up during any of these times and a price I paid.
Exhausted from rules and never having a voice,
Cost so much in my life because I had no choice.
Perhaps I played by the rules until I was grown,
That the rules of the game became my own.
I lost myself in the rules that didn't include me,
They kept down a people who shared my history.
If I couldn't stand up and motivate myself,
How could I expect this from anyone else?
I had to face the demons that were staring me down,
And tell them to back off and get the hell out of town.
Because I had to speak and I did it with grace,
And for those who didn't want to hear me go to your own space.
Since I will be talking from this day forward,
The only thing that could cease me would be the Lord.
I will never be silenced for this is my day,
And if you can't handle my voice then get out the way!

IDENTITY

BLACK TIES

You refer to him as an African-American or Black man,
But look at him as a man that is doing the very best he can.
He has been challenged for hundreds of years,
And has suffered so many blood, sweat and tears.
He is not a criminal nor is he lazy,
And could be construed as sometimes crazy.
But if you've been beaten and broken down,
By a society that sometimes denounces brown.
You may be provoked to do something wrong,
But you have to think and try and be strong.
The color of skin should never be a reason,
To lynch a man during any season.
For he is a father, brother and friend,
A major source for some to depend.
You too would be angry if the world challenged you,
To stay in a place that is required by few.
You know the history and have read all the books,
Of the struggles of this man and the things that he took.
He has come of age and no longer plays with a toy,
He has been disrespected and referred to as boy.
Take a look at the man and as you are staring,
Look at the individual and stop comparing.
For he should be judged by his own actions,
Instead of the worlds negative reactions.
And when people continue to stereotype,
Tell them to back off and don't believe the hype!
For some of history has been built on lies,
But all of his dedication is to his Black Ties!

KNOW YOUR HISTORY

Pain, sorrow, degradation, humiliation and discrimination,

Are hard words to hear from even the strongest people in civilization.

Yes, we were slaves and slaves we were but nonetheless we were great,

Our ancestors' survived nightmares as others determined their fate.

We speak of our history in painful terms that are hard to get over,

We can't discuss the pain while drunk or sober.

We have let our history become something that was bad,

What happened to our people has made us mad.

But who are we to give up so easily because of that pain,

For we shouldn't bow down to anyone because we have no shame.

Yes, our forefathers were beaten, tied up and burned,

But that is the reason why our hearts should yearn.

We should make sure that their deaths were not in vain,

For we are the offspring that have much to gain.

We should learn from those experiences and make sure we know,

The entire knowledge of our history no matter where we go.

We should fight with knowledge and never pull a trigger,

We should seek respect from all and never be referred to as nigger.

More than 100 years have passed since we were released from slavery,

This is a fact that we all should treasure and always savor.

Even those slaves that waited the additional two years and someone had to seek,

To inform them of their freedom on that hot day June 19th.

We must learn our history and pass it down to our kids,

And one day their children will ask what we did.

We must prove to the world that throughout the years,

That we built two continents on our blood, sweat and tears.

So don't be ashamed of that great, great-grandfather that burned in his boots,

Be proud of the family that would give their lives to continue your roots!

MISS AFRICAN-AMERICAN

Look up, stand straight and let the world know who you are,
For you have come a long way baby and you're a bright shining star.

You are strong, elegant, vibrant, respected and bold,
You are what your mother expected and worth your weight in gold.

Nina Simone told us that you are young, gifted and black,
And if this is every disputed you are prepared to attack.

Attack in the sense of fighting with your brain,
Because you are smart and talented but never insane.

Talk the talk and walk the walk and never let yourself down,
Show the world that you are Miss African-
American in all shades of brown.

So lift up your head, put on a smile and
strut the stuff yo' mama gave you,
And let the world know that God made you a
woman of not one continent but two!

LEGACY

Work hard, take chances and make some decisions,

Be vibrant, be strong and live out your visions.

You see we worked hard and took some chances,

In spite of the barriers and our circumstances.

There were times we were killed and other times enslaved,

But yet we persevered and now paths we have paved.

Just imagine a people that have gone through so much,

Physical, mental and emotional abuse but the lives they still touch.

Used by others to produce their goods,

Not earning a living but did the best they could.

Lets dig a little deeper and let the story be told,

We were people used as chattel and yes, we were sold!

Men, children and women on an auction block, no this didn't fit her,

Being purchased to breed more slaves to the highest bidder.

Some of them revolted because they had to be free,

At times they were caught and were hung from a tree.

Yes, hung for no reason, no suicide, no note,

Hung from a tree simply because they wanted to vote.

As times moved on some things changed but there was still fear,

Trying to sit at a lunch counter but being told, "You can't sit here!"

Some wanted to play sports, sing, act and yes, be educated,

But every step of the way our fate was debated.

Someone always made decisions about where we should be,

The problem about the people was they looked nothing like me.

Every time we tried to speak up it was the power we lacked,

Being told you have no voice simply because you were black.

We never gave up and though we have a ways to go,

The experiences our people encountered should make us grow.

Whether rich and famous or someone in the community,

The approaches taken should bring some unity.

For the tracks that are made is for others to follow,

Not just yesterday or today but also tomorrow.

The path that has been paved started way back then,

You see they left the door open so we could walk right in.

Because of them you can be all that you can be,

They lived; they died and left us this legacy.

FAMILY

CHILD'S PLAY

Run, jump, slide and play as much as you can,
Have the time of your life and keep fun in your plan.
Wear the current fashion trends, yes, all the latest fads,
 Always think positive, let the world know you're bad!
When you go to school every day make good grades,
B's look pretty good but the best grades are A's.
While riding on the school bus check out the view,
You may see a positive billboard that could one day be you.
You are a child with dreams, dreams that could come true,
But you must follow those dreams for they are accomplished by few.
Take those dreams one day at a time, they will make sense,
For they are the dreams for you and your parents.
And when you are grown and well on you way,
You'll know that those dreams were more than Child's Play.

FAMILY

Families bring a number of issues which we all may reject,

For if you live within each other there are things we should expect.

Family members may steal, deceive, hate, debate, make you irate and play games,

It's hard to believe but this has been many families claim to fame.

You are one and one you will be because God made everyone a family,

When the seed was planted no one knew who would be on the tree.

But once you were born and grew up you understood that blood was thicker than water,

Although this was not your choice it was the ingredients that the good Lord ordered.

And tell me who will question what God has put first,

For he made the choice of your family before your birth.

Families argue, disagree, fall out and yes they sometimes fight,

But family will also mend you to health and stay with you during the night.

They sometimes treat friends and strangers better than they do each other,

They take the sides of others as if they were their mother.

The fact remains that they know who their family members are,

No matter how much they're apart they're never really far.

If you could change your family would you really take that risk and why?

To end up in the same place with someone else who could also make you cry.

Remember the people you love may hurt you the most,

But the love they have for you as family is one that you could boast.

Why try to conquer the family unit in which God has made,

No one forced your hand or has asked you to stay.

You stay because you love the family in which you were born,

Not everyday of the week but if you leave you would be torn.

They will make sure you're safe and never give up on you,

They will cheer you on in whatever you pursue.

Give back to your family, those in which you love,

You get strength when you're down that fits tight as a glove.

And when you think they've abandoned you and left your side,

Just turn and look up the block and you'll see them stopping by.

You will always have some dismay but you'll also have fun,

To be part of a family unit where you're all considered one.

FAMILY REUNION

Fried chicken, potato salad, spaghetti, ribs, hot links and many other things,

Whew, the food is so good especially when mama put her foot in those greens.

As you look around whether it's in July, August or September,

You cherish every moment being with your family members.

You take time to reunite with your family while remembering the past,

Thinking of those that have passed on but you know how memories do last.

Seeing your cousins, uncles, aunts and of course the new babies,

Thinking how this family began from a God fearing man and a great lady.

You see they started it all from the time the first child was born,

Then that child grew up and the story goes on and on.

Some memories are great and some may bring grief,

But it was through the family that gave us relief.

Remember the days when Grandma would say,

Lord watch over my babies in a very special way.

Even though you know how much she loves you and if you got out of line,

She would say get in this house because your butt is mine.

Don't play so hard and end up staying out too late at night,

You know your mamas gonna get you if you're not in before the street light.

Family means so much and when you all come together,

You reestablish your history in any type of weather.

Being born into a family gives you privileges I hope you know,

If you don't realize that now you will as you grow.

For all the things that go wrong in life and some things we may lack,

When you raise your head from despair you notice the family has your back.

You may not see many of them while on your journey from day to day,

They may live in other cities but they're just a phone call away.

You don't have to wait for that one time a year to see how they are,

Pick up a phone, write a letter or visit the family that's not far.

And another idea that doesn't take research,

Take some time and meet each other at a nearby Church.

So make your plans, keep the faith and provide your opinion,

So everyone will have a great time during the Family Reunion.

SHE IS

She endured the pain and gave the gift of life to her children,

she is a **MOTHER.**

She provided spiritual guidance to those near and far,

she is a **GODMOTHER.**

She instilled pride, she is a guide, she stands by your side,

she is an **AUNT.**

She took time to praise and lead you in the right direction,

she is a **SISTER.**

She is there for you when no one else is around,

she is a **FRIEND.**

She said, "Don't judge anyone until you have walked a mile in their shoes,"

she is a **MENTOR.**

She knew you could be whatever you wanted to be in life…

if you wanted it bad enough.

She may not have good street direction but…

she knows the way to salvation.

She can't always stop the downpour but…

she can take a walk in the rain with you.

She would often cry for others in pain but…

would hide her own troubles.

She is one of the above or maybe a few, **she is** loving,

generous and close to perfect…**SHE IS YOU.**

SPECIAL OCCASIONS

DAD

He rises everyday to make ends meet,
He sits on the bus but will give up his seat.
He knows how to make it no matter what,
He'll make sure you're ok with no if, ands or buts.
He's strong, vibrant, calm and cool,
He uses his brain as a tool.
He shows us that a family is built on affection,
Even though he sometimes lack some direction.
To keep his family going he'll walk a mile,
To see his kids bright, shining smile.
He's been demeaned in his life,
But refuses to give up on his wife.
He has followed before but has become a leader,
He's learned so much though not a reader.
He's bronze, masculine, regal and tall,
He's also dark and sometimes small.
No matter what he is I am always glad,
To know this King whom I call Dad!

HAPPY FATHER'S DAY…
TO MY MOTHER!

I'm not confused when I speak of my mother,

On Father's Day for there is no other.

She has played the role since my birth,

That's a long time on this earth.

She did not choose this title for it chose her,

To be the male in my life but don't call her Sir.

She has measured up against all men in this life,

She has dealt with the hard times, struggles and strife.

She has made me realize that life is too short,

To linger on the hard times and to abort.

The children you birth become your own,

Even if you raise them all alone.

You make the best out of any bad situation,

A great life for your family is your final destination.

Love your children and they'll love you back,

Even if a male is what your home lacks.

Make peace with yourself and continue to strive,

To support your children and to stay alive.

Teach them in the way in which they should live,

Make sure they are Godly and willing to give.

Your children won't forget you in anyway,

They'll give honor to you on Father's Day!

MOTHER

We celebrate mothers on Mother's Day,
The things they've done during one day in May.
Although this day is taken so dear,
Celebrate your mom throughout the year.
Your mother is the reason you've made it so far,
She taught you to love people for who they are.
Do all you can do for the ones you love,
And leave the rest to God above.
It took a long time but you understand her caring,
She takes care of everyone and believes in sharing.
Watching her as a child there was no one greater,
For a mother to feed her children and she would eat later.
No matter what happened she put all of her children first,
There was enough food for you until you could burst.
She wasn't rich but she gave you the best,
She nourished all of you like a bird in a nest.
Only your mother can tell you what it's been like in her life,
Some very good times but some struggles and strife.

On this mother's day please shout out loud,
In honor of your mother and how she made you proud.
She makes the world a better place and that's how it goes,
You can feel her presence from your head to your toes.

WORDS OF ENCOURAGEMENT

DECISIONS

Eyebrows may raise and concerns may arise,

I'm asking some questions so don't be surprised.

Have you ever made decisions that could determine your fate?

But by the time you realized the mistake it was much too late.

Have you ever had a reason to want to stop and cry?

No matter who was present or as people walked by.

You were young and in love and that made you feel good,

You cherished a person and did all that you could.

Your heart may have been fine and filled with joy,

But in a matter of minutes that joy is no more.

You loved someone so hard but they betrayed your trust,

They made your heart heavy because their actions were unjust.

The pressure to make love because of the way you felt,

Has turned to bitterness because you saw them with someone else.

Why should you let someone steal your joy at your expense?

Such an attitude of deception and ultimate intransigence.

Perhaps you didn't see it coming like a robber in the night,

Your lover took your soul and now they're clear out of sight.

The camaraderie you had from your very first date,

Made you think this person could be your soul mate.

But this has all changed and as you well know,

Hearts can be broken if you allow someone to do so.

So don't make a temporary decision for a permanent situation,

Because the love you sought could be mere infatuation.

You may have been told that you were their one and only,

But as time goes on it was better to be lonely.

You made a decision to have sex from the attention you were receiving,

But love mirrors so many things and looks can be deceiving.

By the time you knew what happened the love you knew turned to hate,

But you gave all you had when you had sex instead of just date.

You didn't really know the person and now you're hurt and ashamed,

You search for relief and others to blame.

The consequences could be deadly and you could get Aids,

So make the right decision because it could extend your days.

Try to learn all you can about HIV, AIDS and other things you don't know,

Once you arm yourself with knowledge it's with you wherever you go.

Confide in your parents, teachers or pastor for decisions that may
come your way,

But for anything you deal with in life make sure you pray.

And if all fails or may seem too hard,

Let it all go and hand it over to God!

I'VE BEEN IN THE
STORM TOO LONG

You may hear some people say, "I've been in the storm too long,"

But in spite of their struggles they continue to be strong.

So many terrible things have happened in the world, yet we are still sane,

But the devastation that hit August 28, 2005 was a fierce hurricane.

People in the South were told that it would be bad so this they knew,

But who would have known the major damage that was due.

As the hurricane moved in it got up to 175 miles per hour,

First the wind, then the rain and out went the power.

Yes, the power that controls the light switches, TV's and things,

But the people lacked power also and the resources power brings.

People began to think, "Oh my God, what will we do?"

They looked at their children but their options were few.

The rain continued to flow and then the levees broke,

People were homeless and stranded and then Mayor Nagin spoke.

He pleaded for the Government to immediately step in,

He questioned why it took so long and where had they been.

The people that were Americans just a few days before,

Were now referred to as refugees, evacuees and more.

How could something like this happen in the Land of the Free,

Where resources are plentiful and you can "be all you can be."

People began to question if this was about race or class,

Please ask those questions later but for now move your ass.

Get the people to safety, provide some assistance and I'll do the same,

Then once they are safe and secure then continue to blame.

We look and listen to the media and everyday we have cried,

For the people that are homeless and for all those who have died.

To understand the big picture you must look back in time and you have to be wise,

You have to understand your history and see things in your forefather's eyes.

When you think of New Orleans you think about Mardi Gra and how much fun it brings,

Mississippi brings the unforgettable Delta Blues and when cotton was king.

Yes, I said, cotton because it was part of the South as you all know,

I could add in the Civil War, Grandfather Clauses and Jim Crow.

You see it's all connected and as we look back,

We are a strong people but it is power we lack.

We have come a long way but we have a long way to go,

We must educate our children and tell them what we know.

Hurricane Katrina reminded some that all men may not be created equal even today,

You can work hard, learn just as much but you're different in every way.

You can read about the tribulations of slavery and how they did strive,

Beaten, raped, tortured, demeaned and a people demoralized.

These are the reasons that this event cannot keep you down,

You must remember the struggles of a people and remove the frown.

Your Grand mamma may have told you to hold on to Jesus,

Because he is the only one that truly loves you and could please us.

So yes, you've been in the storm too long and it's not over yet so move on with force,

Dry your eyes, stand tall, teach your children and stay on your course.

WE ALL FALL DOWN

One day I was Falling and I couldn't get up no matter how hard I tried,
I cried out loud for anyone but it was like the world had died.
My screams got louder and I began to ramble,
The world around me was in total shambles!
The people I knew were falling too,
We couldn't help each other and didn't know what to do.
It was apparently clear of our constant grief,
What was happening to us was disbelief.
How could we all fall in such a powerful place,
Where freedom was plentiful and you had your own space.
We had all hit rock bottom and life was not good,
We lived day to day but not as good as we could.
Some gave up while others continued to strive,
It took a lot of work but you could be revived.
The days, weeks, months, years continued to move on,
There was no relief in sight and the good life was gone.
Stop! Think about what I just said,
The good life is gone, that I dread!
Look at your life and all you've gone through,
It will be over if you believe it is true.
But if you believe you can make it despite the trials,
You'll make others believe and they'll pray in the aisles.
So don't give up because the struggles won't last,
Just focus on your goals and think of your past.
Sometimes you may fall but you can overcome your plight,
But you must push forward and never give up the fight!

MUSIC
SOOTHES THE SOUL!

Music soothes the soul and releases good feelings,
It penetrates the room from the floor to the ceiling.
Music changes the way you see everything in life,
It makes a man turn a girlfriend into his wife.
Listen to the sound of Superstar,
Luther belts it out while in your car.
Some music is fast while other music is slow,
It turns dry land into water that flow.
Music can transpose a weary heart,
It lightens your load and gives a great start.
Lay back and relax and while closing your eyes,
Reflect on the sounds of days gone by.
Music boosts your soul in everyway,
When you hear the sounds of Marvin Gaye.
Whether music is rap, gospel or old school,
You can jam to the beat and appear to be cool.
Dance fast, slow dance or maybe even step,
And if you can't keep up someone will intercept.
Music can make a bad day disappear,
It soothes the soul and is good to the ear.
So the next time you're down and feeling blue,
Dance to a song or perhaps even two.

SMELL THE FLOWERS

Rush, rush, rush everyday is faster than the last,

You never slow down and your future will soon be your past.

You may not know it but there is power in a flower,

The look, the smell is truly flower power.

Even if you don't believe this just take a look,

Look at a flower in a yard or even in a book.

Flowers can change your outlook on life,

This can be testified by any husband or wife.

Flowers can change doom and gloom,

This can be verified when entering a room.

Flowers can make you smile or cry,

And no one will ever question why.

You must be prepared when approaching one,

They change your emotions and work well with sun.

So take time to smell the flowers each and every hour,

It could be a picture or a garden because they all have power.

SPIRITUAL CORNER

IN MY FATHER'S HOUSE

There are many mansions for the Bible tells me so,

Yes, this is a scripture that everyone should know.

If you aren't aware that this Father's house is the place to be,

Perhaps not at this time but later in life you'll see.

He's made a place where we are all welcome and wanted,

For this is a house trimmed in gold and is never haunted.

Make this your destiny for his house is your home,

A place to dwell forever and where you'll never be alone.

You don't have to pay rent and there is no mortgage to pay,

You never have to move out and it's the perfect place to pray.

You don't have bills to pay and you'll never be homeless,

You'll think to yourself, "Oh my God I'm Blessed!"

In order to be a resident in this house there is a price,

You have to be redeemed and accept the Lord Christ.

You have to be obedient and know you have been redeemed,

And if you're ever in doubt make sure to read John 14.

John 14:1-3 Let not your heart be troubled: ye believe in God, believe also in me. In my Father's house are many mansions: if it were not so, I would have told you. I go to prepare a place for you. And if I prepare a place for you, I will come again, and receive you unto myself; that where I am, there ye may be also.

DIVERSITY

THE DIVERSITY CHALLENGE

Working very hard from day to day,
Always listening to what peers had to say.
Sometimes to exhausted to eat at night,
Being part of the team was the biggest plight.

One day another catch word surfaced the scene,
Being told it would not be "lip service" if you know what I mean.
Would it be treated like the others and soon disappear,
The training was due so it would become more clear.

Diversity, diversity was the new word on the street,
Like all the other catchwords would there be defeat?
Things were changing all the time so they knew it would leave,
Many would soon ignore diversity and they'll all be relieved.

Being told it's just not about black and white,
Yeah, diversity would work and it'll be accepted with delight.
But what about all the differences we share in our life,
Who wants to listen to someone's struggles and strife?

The times are changing and we will soon see,
That valuing differences in everyone is the key.
This is not an attempt to start some confusion,
Only an opportunity to foster inclusion.

It's not a hard task to include someone that is not like you,
You'll see from your own eyes there is a clearer view.
And a lesser task to get to know different ways of doing things,
Appreciating new ways and the joy it brings.

So look around the world and let others know,
That there are differences in all of us wherever we go.
Not just the differences you can see but others as well,
Those differences you can't see will be dispelled.

Challenge yourself to respect differences in everyone you meet,
This is not a major race so there is no defeat.
Look beyond race and gender and establish rapport,
Start a new way of thinking that you'll like more and more!

TEACHING DIVERSE STUDENTS

Teaching for many, many years has been my claim to **fame,**

A subject matter expert in a course that remains the **same.**

I have little time for camaraderie so I always move on with **force,**

I need all the instruction time to present the material for my **course.**

The students had to read a chapter prior to arriving for **class,**

If all my questions are answered I knew that would be a **blast.**

Another new class on this first day of **school,**

We review the syllabus and the campus **rules.**

As I prepare to teach my course I really look at my **class,**

The class is like a rainbow much different than years **past.**

Some major differences in most students' **face,**

Will this require adjustment to my teaching **pace?**

I immediately asked a question and a white student raised her **hand,**

Well, this was not new that she had an answer since she was on familiar **land.**

I had another question and as I approached an Indian student's **desk,**

Fear came over the students face as though this were the final **test.**

Was it because his culture was quiet and learned by **observation,**

Perhaps this was the reason for his apparent **reservation.**

Two black students that sat in the back appeared to be on their **own,**

They looked as though they knew the answers but just wanted to be left **alone.**

As I turned in the other direction a Hispanic student clear in **sight,**

Her mannerisms appeared to be a positive force so I knew she would get it **right.**

But when she realized I was walking toward her and started to give her a **look,**

She immediately changed her course and started to read her **book.**

Since no one had any answers I decided to look through the class **roster,**

I could barely pronounce any of the names they differed from Smith or **Foster.**

As I stood and looked around the room I had to change my course of **action,**

Did this new student population require some sort of **passion?**

I stopped and thought for a second and took a step **back,**

Perhaps I needed to revamp my style or was it compassion I **lacked.**

I'd heard about breaking the ice and didn't want my class to go through **reductions,**

So I noticed smiles and eye contact when announced we would start **introductions.**

If you intend to teach the students today just remember the multicultural **population,**

Because getting to know them initially could really boost your **reputation.**

DEARLY DEPARTED

R
E
M
E
M
B
E
R

M
E

Loving, caring, smart, diligent and a wonderful friend,

A person who was all of that and someone you could depend.

Sometimes a presence that was like the quiet whisper of a bird,

A mellow song in the wind but could always be heard.

Working so very hard to make sure the family was secure,

No matter what would happen honesty was pure.

A person who loved being with family through struggles or strife,

No matter the situation it was handled in life.

Children reflect all they see and more,

They cherished the person and what they stood for.

Someone who meant so much to others and when they walked in the door,

You knew you encountered quality and someone you could adore.

No one will ever forget this person because they all know,

The path they have followed and why they all glow.

So don't drop your head because you are all proud,

To be part of this person's life, so shout out loud!

They may not be with us on this day,

But if they were here, here's what they'd say.

"Please don't be discouraged,

For I loved you and be of good courage.

I won't ask a lot from you but all I ask is that you never forget,

The good and hard times we all shared but we never quit.

You see where I am now there is no pain,

I have eternal life and even more to gain.

I know it's hard to understand and the truth remains to be seen,

But to validate this fact just read John 14.

So lift up your heads and please don't cry,

Don't question the Lord and never ask, Why!

Just know that I love you and that will always be,

All I want is your love and for you to Remember Me!"

STOP!

WHAT WILL IT TAKE?

What will it take to realize that women and girls are murdered every **hour**?
By someone who loved and cherished them but the love turned to **power**.
What will it take to stop the screams that we've all heard in the **night**?
Of a man beating his wife from dusk to **daylight**.
What will it take to overcome the numerous bruises that everyone can **see**?
Will it be the local government for they are the powers that **be**?
What will it take to have life, liberty and the pursuit of **happiness**?
The inalienable rights that many women and girls **miss**.
Growing up in a world believing that you could live like **June Clever**,
Dressed up to walk around the house and serve Ward, Wally and the **Beaver**.
Perhaps June knew her place and would never step out of **line**,
Being beautiful was her role but beauty decreases with **time**.
Was June ever hit, demeaned and brutally beaten by **Ward**?
Perhaps we'll never know because she only told the **Lord**.
Lights, cameras, action and make sure you read your **script**,
Perhaps the words didn't flow well because of her swollen **lip**.
I'll leave June alone now because that was all **TV**,
She could have experienced mental abuse, abuse you can't **see**.
Now, back to reality and staying on the **course**,
It's hard to get results when you have no **voice**.
What will it take for someone to hear my **screams**?
Would it take a spotlight with an exuberant **beam**?
Will it take a witness to hear my **cries**?
To stand by my side when he tells the **lies**.

Will it take more men to go through **abuse**?

To spark their interest before they blow a **fuse**.

Will it take the community to stand against the **violence**?

To address the male counterparts and their ultimate **intransigence**.

Will it take more money and leaders to silence the **shouts**?

That will save women and girls and to stomp violence **out**.

As the cycle of violence continues to **grow**,

We loose millions of women, God bless their **souls**.

The physical, mental and emotional **devastation**,

Can't be compared to an argument or minor **frustration**.

Stop! Stop! Stop! Someone please hear my **cry**!

Before I'm another statistic that had to **die**!

For I died long ago from the first blow to my **head**!

I'm walking around daily but I'm the living **dead**!

Will it take an act of nature to send out roars of **thunder**?

Or will it take the silent witnesses who are all six feet **under**?

Can the violence be stopped! What will it take for us to be **free**?

As I look in the mirror, it may take **me**!

WOMEN

WOMEN!

WOMEN! Degradation, humiliation, separation
and discrimination are things we have shared,

We suffered for so many years of all this
injustice and thought no one cared.

We have conformed, reformed and been
denied access to the skills we lacked,

Amongst our own peers we were demeaned
and no one ever had our back.

We have been on the battlefield without suits of honor that fit,

Sometimes we were casualties of war but we never quit.

We have been abused and many victims have looked just like me,

Seeking support by the judicial system has not made us free.

We have come to believe that the world looked at us as being weak,

We have been restricted to the minimum
and not the pleasures we seek.

The main problem is the fact that we have ideas, joys and sorrow,

We have provided for our children's today and tomorrow.

We have been afraid to speak up and
sometimes we never took a stand,

We have been compared to others like us
but rarely compared to a man.

Living in a world built on being dependent upon by someone else,

But we're staying in the game even though
these were the cards we were dealt.

We are making our mark on this place called a democracy,

And when the world takes notice they'll look up and see me.

For we are not victims by any means of the word,

We are strong, we are diligent, and we will be heard.

We have been stereotyped to be weak and only to whine,

But the forces that we charge will someday be mine.

We won't sit back and cry as many will believe,

We will push forward, not backwards, and we will achieve.

For we are women and yes, watch us roar,

Like a tigress in the night or like a bird we'll soar.

So don't underestimate our abilities for we will shock you,

When you see our moves and all the things we can do.

So many before us have taken the challenge and stayed in the race,

By fighting for women's rights and keeping the pace.

Woman have been brutalized and condemned but we won't fear.

We will strive for equality, justice and we'll persevere.

Not having support may have been our plight,

But it won't keep us down during the fight.

So the next time you see us taking a stand,

Don't sit back and judge us just **GIVE US A HAND!**

JUST BECAUSE
YOU'RE YOU

IN APPRECIATION OF YOU!

You rush everyday just to make ends meet,

You're tired as can be but you won't claim defeat.

Stretching yourself thin as each day goes on,

Life's been this way since you were born.

But you never give up even though days are hard,

The stress over comes you and you've played your last card.

We think about you and no matter how hard you strive,

It's good to be blessed and to be alive.

Our lives are so busy and we don't take the time to spell the flowers,

Life passes us by as if a day were an hour.

We have gone through so much and there's a long haul,

For peace in this world you make the next call.

You know what makes you happy so focus on that,

Make things happen in your life, it's your turn at bat.

People look for things in life that will bring them wealth,

But the greatest gift from God is to be in good health.

So look within your heart, deep down in your soul,

Finding complete happiness should be your goal.

You're part of our life and let the story be told,

That you're such a good person with a heart like gold.

So if anything bothers you don't live life with worry,

Smell the roses everyday because there's no big hurry.

Take time, recognize that you get one life, not two,

So we're celebrating just because you're you.

Stop! Think about it before you make your next move,

You see life is so precious so get in the groove.

Wake everyday with thoughts of blessings and a smile,

With a positive mind you could walk a mile.

Despite all the curve balls life throws you life is not a mess,

It's difficult and hard but we are blessed.

For we are blessed to know God and then to know you,

This is in appreciation of you and all that you do.

FOR THE HOME

ON HER SIDE

When you enter this room you will find peace,
This is where all friction stops and problems cease.
You can freshen up in so many ways,
Or prepare your clothes for several days.
You'll notice in minutes that this room is blessed,
It's the perfect place for you to get dressed.
The mirrors in this room reflects who you are,
For in this room you're a shining star.
When you go in this room there is so much to be done,
But when you exit you are number one.
You will be transitioned in just an hour,
With brushing and combing and a nice warm shower.
You will meet the world and they'll like what they see,
Because your transitioned beauty will set you free.

ON HIS SIDE

The male in this room can take his time,

To prepare for the day and just unwind.

He can shave for the day and pamper himself,

Thinking of his day and his potential wealth.

For life can be difficult if you don't start your day here,

In this midst of the shower there is no need to fear.

So pull out your towels and your shaving stuff,

And if you're strong in your manhood use a powder puff.

Because it's all about you when you arrive in this place,

You enjoy the time alone and all of the space.

THIS THRONE!

Isn't every room in a house considered great?
Perhaps this question is up for debate.
Privacy is granted and you will tell,
You can read, think or talk on your cell.
From toddlers, teens and when you are grown,
You are the head of this room when you sit on this throne.

Welcome!

Welcome! Is the word you're always hear from us,
We'll talk and laugh but will never fuss.
We enjoy your presence each time you enter our home,
You'll enjoy the camaraderie and will never feel alone.
For laughter is the key to a happy environment,
Not anger, sadness or any resentment.
So come in, rest yourself and have a bite to eat,
And if you are tired lift up your feet.
For this house is fully blessed and for all who enters,
Will feel the warmth in the summer, spring, fall and winter.

NEW BEGINNING

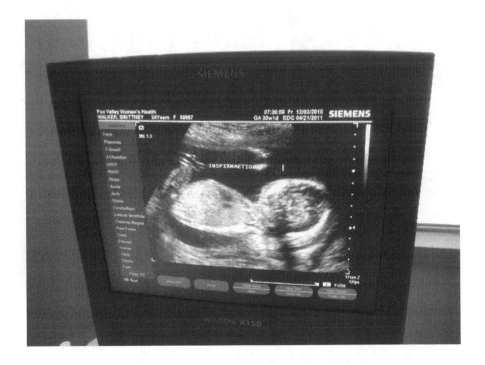

THE END

Hard times in your life seem like they are never done,
But you have to realize that life is no dry run.
Take life one step at a time, then a day and a year,
Times may be difficult but you must face your fear.
Face life head on and reflect on your family and a friend,
Live each day and be happy for this is never the end!

The Beginning…